The Joy of Being Me

Being the Person He Created Me to Be

N e s s i e   M a c

Contents

Preface

" Mum, I don't think I'll live beyond Christmas." My heart broke for my 16-year-old daughter who was so desperately sad. She felt that she didn't have anything to live for. Safeguarding referrals had been made and we were again seeking the help of professionals. She no longer smiled, instead preferring to stay in her bedroom when she was at home. What was a mother to do? For me the only thing I could do was pray, although there were times when I couldn't manage it – I just wept for her instead. It was then my friends prayed and lifted up my cries. My poor beautiful daughter.

The one good thing was that she was going to college a few days a week. During the summer, her consultant didn't think she would ever get there. But there, at college, she was making friends and broadening her horizons. But this wasn't enough. I felt she had so much to live for, but she just couldn't see it.

I used to wonder what people meant when they said they were gripped by fear. And at that moment I knew. Fear gripped my throat. It gripped my heart. I sometimes found it hard to breath. I would go out and always be in a hurry to get back to her, never knowing what I would find. I had to trust God. Who else did I have?

And then one day my daughter said, "Mum, next year…" and I realised that I had been holding my breath all this time. Now I knew she was looking forward and was making plans, and I silently rejoiced. She had put herself in the future.

My mother also put my young son Micah in the future – I was told that he would never walk, let alone run. But one day many years ago my mum said, "Last night I had a dream, and I could see Micah running." I kept hold of that Vision and now my son is a professional actor and dancer. He is now planning to release a single record – that's putting himself in the future. And it's a future bright with promise. Not the one predicted way back when he had to wear special boots to support his legs.

My youngest daughter wasn't expected to live, and because her brain didn't receive enough oxygen or blood flow for a period of time when she was born, she had hypoxic ischemic encephalopathy grade 3 as well as other complications. (HIE is a form of brain damage that can kill the neurons that transfer motor signals.) Even three years later it makes me sad to read her neonatal discharge summary. The professionals have said her future could be challenging, but I know that through God all things are possible.

CHAPTER 1

The End – Alpha

Why start at the end? Because God always starts with the end in mind. When He sent His Son, God knew it would end with the defeat of satan. God knew Paul would finish the course set before him. And He sees you as you are going to be – not as you are now.

This is the Vision that He has for you: "to be perfect and complete in Him" (Colossians 2:10). And because you have been created in His image (Genesis 1:27), the Vision He has for you resides within you as well. But you may ask, does that mean that I am just the same as everyone else? Yes, we are the same… and then again we're not. Just as snow is made up of individual flakes that are all unique, so each and every one of us is different. God's Vision for each of us is different and unique.

The Bible says, "Eye has not seen, nor ear heard, nor have entered into the heart of man, the things which God has prepared for those who love Him" (1 Corinthians 2:10). However, you will need to find out what these things are. As the scripture goes on to say, "But God has revealed them to us through His Spirit. For the Spirit searches all things, yes, the deep things of God." "...and these things have been freely given to us by God" (1 Corinthians 2:11-12). I believe that God has created you for a purpose and therefore you already have all the attributes that you need. But these attributes need to be revealed, just like a diamond. A diamond is formed deep within the Earth's mantle around 100 miles from the surface. Under enormous pressure and immense heat, the gem will begin to form from carbonate rocks such as limestone, marble and dolomite. Next, forces within the Earth bring the diamond to the surface. Yet, rough as it is, if it is a gem it will be picked out for its form and value. In the same way, you have been selected because, "Everyone who is called by My name, whom I have created for My glory; I have formed him, yes, I have made him" (Isaiah 43:7).

God has made so many promises to you – you only have to read His word to find them. He says, "But if any of you lacks wisdom, let him ask of God, who gives to all liberally and without reproach, and it will be given to him" (James 1:5). Just ask Him. You will find that His promises are not hidden from us but rather *for* us. Jeremiah 29:11 says, "For I know the plans I have for you, declares the Lord, plans for welfare and not for evil, to give you a future and a hope." One of my favourite verses of all times is Zephaniah 3:17, where it says "The Lord your God is with you, He is mighty to save. He will take great delight in you, He will quiet you with his love, He will rejoice over you with singing." Wow! He looks at me and rejoices! I believe that is because He looks at us as we are going to be rather than what we are. When we look at ourselves, we can get so disappointed, so busy looking at our circumstances and the people around us and the people who have gone before us. We sometimes even look at people younger than we are, seeing them with so much to live for and our lives might appear to pale in comparison. We need to stop this. We need to start believing that God has something in store for us. Something so great that it causes Him to rejoice. Isn't it wonderful to know that He knew us from our mother's womb? He knows the very hairs on our head. He loves us with such an everlasting love (Psalm 139:13).

I remember when I first became a Christian, 26 years ago now. I had felt so unloved for most of my life – I knew my family and friends loved me, but I didn't *feel* love. To this day I don't know why. When I found that God loved me unconditionally it changed my whole life. To be loved without conditions attached is not something most of us are used to. And in addition to knowing that someone has a plan for us – a plan not to cause harm but to better us – is so reassuring. To know that He has gone before us and made the crooked paths straight (Isaiah 45:2). There is nothing He can't do. Nothing is impossible for Him. We have it in writing in His words. The Bible says that the Spirit brings back to remembrance what we have read, but if we are not reading the Bible He has nothing to bring back to us. It's as simple as that. Like we feed our physical bodies every day, we should be feeding our spiritual bodies as well. We need to be strong for the tasks that He has set out before us each day.

Do you know we can only become what we already are? For example, a son or daughter may train to become a surgeon because that is what his or her parents want, but deep down he or she might know that they want to be an artist – they feel that this is their true calling. So that is how we need to see ourselves – not as we are now. Imagine you want to lose weight because you see yourself as unhealthy and fat. Even though you may well be, this will not help at all. The mind is powerful, and if we knew how powerful it is then there are many things we wouldn't say, let alone think. We need to remember that we need to renew our mind daily (Romans 12:2) and that life and death is in the power of the tongue (Proverbs 18:21). So instead, try visualising yourself as slim. I believe that one of the best ways to reach your goals is to think of yourself as a slim healthy person. Always ask yourself the question, what would a healthy person do? Would a healthy person eat three burgers and chips for breakfast washed down by a milkshake? No, didn't think so. You would want something that is going to be healthy for your body, which after all is a temple of the living God.

Or what if you wanted to have better control of your finances? You may want to save for the future or have more money to give to good causes. Whatever the reason, you need to start with a budget. Some people think that a budget only tells you to stop spending, but if done correctly a budget will tell you what you can have.

I believe that having a Vision puts you in the future with God. We all have so much to give to ourselves and others. Don't let this life pass you by without you accomplishing that which you were tasked to do.

I pray that this small book will have a big impact on your life because as you read it, I pray that God will reveal to you the '*You He created you to be,*' and that will have the biggest impact on *your* life.

CHAPTER 2

God: The Master Visionary

An expert can pick out a gem amongst a pile of rough diamonds. To extend the analogy, what makes you special? The answer is God's Vision within you. That is what makes you unique. Yet just like a rough diamond waiting to be transformed into a unique gem, there will be many facets to the Vision. But without Vision these facets will be hidden and you will not shine with the brilliance that God intended. For, "Where there is no vision, the people perish" (Proverbs 28:19).

This means that if we do not fulfil the Vision God has called us to be we perish inwardly and our lives remain unfulfilled. God called us to be productive, which means that good fruit must flourish in every part of our lives. You may even now be thinking, "God would never give me a Vision," but why not?

When my son was 12, he asked me what I had wanted to be when I grew up. I couldn't tell him. You know why? Because I never knew myself. Instead, I drifted into one thing after another. When I finished my secondary education I went to college then secretarial school. From there I drifted from job to job with no clear destination in mind – if it felt good, I did it. So, I became a secretary, sold encyclopaedias door-to-door, became a croupier in a casino and sold handmade jewellery on a market stall at Greenwich Market. In between these jobs I even worked for an All Ladies minicab company – to this day I don't know how I got into that! What I'm saying is that having no clear course in my life meant that I never knew where I was going.

We can all dream of our how we feel our life will play out – our chosen career path, the type of house we might live in, the places we would visit, who we would marry and then how many children we would have, or not! The vast amount of money we would make. And for me it included the many books I would have published. But to dream is not enough – we need a Vision, but not just any Vision. We need the Vision God has for us because God has created us for a unique purpose.

Because He starts with the end in mind, His Vision for you (which He implanted in you) is that you become the person that He created you to be. And if you acknowledge that you have been born for a purpose, then you will be able to focus on what you should be doing. "For we are His workmanship, created in Christ Jesus for good works, which God prepared beforehand that we should walk in them" (Ephesians 2:10).

I believe that this Vision – like a diamond – has more than one facet. The facets of my Vision are, among other things, a wife, a mother, a home educator, an investor, a writer, a foster carer, an active member of my local church, a sister, a daughter, a friend, a student and so much more. These different facets enable my Vision to shine equally brightly in different directions, just like when you hold up a perfectly cut and polished diamond to the light. Yes, all together these facets reflect the 'Me' that He created me to be. And do you know what is so wonderful and exciting? Amazingly our facets can change. I have not always been a mother or wife. But these facets have been added to my Vision.

I believe that God is the Master Visionary and His Vision, formed before time, is to see everyone saved, and each Vision we have been given is part of His great unfolding Vision.

Throughout the Bible we see the evidence of His awesome plan for the world. I believe that the beginning of His unfolding Vision is seen right at the start of creation. God knew that man would fall. He knew that He would need a plan to redeem us from Satan. He knew that only a perfect person could do this. The Vision continues – God had spoken His word and it was going to pass. But it needed the miracle of a virgin birth so that we could see that story unfold. The Bible says that God himself said that "His word would not return to Him void without it having accomplished what He sent it out to perform" (Isaiah 55:11).

We read in Genesis that God made all of creation in six days. Why did He take six days when He could have done it in one? Because there wasn't a 'day' to do it in. First, He had to divide the light from the darkness (Genesis 1:4). So the facets of Vision don't need to be completed in one day, instead you can plan. God planned creation. He took six days and then – seeing it was good – He rested. How did He know it was good? Because it met His expectations! It was what He'd visualised and it had turned out as He'd planned it.

God is the Alpha and the Omega, the beginning and the end. There is nothing that He doesn't know as He is omnipresent. So He knew where He would be on day six of creation. I firmly believe that a Vision puts YOU in the future with God.

Looking at my life I realised that while I was happy, I wasn't fulfilled. I had traded contentment for complacency. As I said, I didn't know what I wanted to be. I don't think I knew who I was. It seemed 'cool' to not know what I wanted to be, or at least it did at the time – big mistake! Whatever came along I did it as long as it felt good. As well as the long list of jobs I mentioned earlier, I even produced a musical with my husband that played at the Broadway Theatre in Barking for four nights. But that's another story for another time!

I even felt I had drifted into my marriage – although it is a happy marriage it wasn't something I thought I would ever do. Now I am not saying that things that just happen are bad. Not at all – I only have to look at my supportive husband and my seven children for that. What I am saying is that having no clear course in my life meant that I never knew where I was going. But there are people in this world who have thought about what they want to be and what they want to do. These people have Vision.

I want to introduce you to some people with Vision, some you know and some, well, you will get to know them just as I have. I believe that Noah was one of the first men who responded to God's call of fulfilling the Vision God had placed in him. We read in Genesis 6:9 that Noah was a righteous man who walked with God. This is an important point to remember. The Earth had become corrupt in God's sight and full of violence. God wanted to destroy it all – the people and the planet. But He actually couldn't. You know why? It is because after He had cursed the serpent in Genesis 14. God said that He had said in Genesis 3:15 that between satan and man's offspring there would be animosity. God's Vision hadn't been fulfilled and if you read the book you know it was because Jesus had yet to fulfil His Vision.

So, God saw how corrupt the Earth had become and that all the people had corrupted their ways. When God said to Noah, "I am going to put an end to all people, for the earth is filled with violence because of them. I am surely going to destroy both them and the earth." So Noah decided to build an ark of cypress wood to fulfil what God had asked of him, and if you don't know the rest of the story you can read all about it in Genesis 6:9 to Genesis 8:22. Noah did as God asked and he saved not only himself, but his family and the animals as well. Vision fulfilled!

And then we read about the apostle Paul in Acts 22:20 where he himself says to God, "And when the blood of Your martyr Stephen was shed, I also was standing by consenting to his death, and guarding the clothes of those who were killing him." He already had a hatred for Christians and he was on his way to have as many killed as possible. He persecuted the church and wanted to destroy it. But then he had an encounter with God and it totally changed him. He went from wanting to destroy the church to saying, "But when it pleased God, who separated me from my mother's womb and called me through His grace, to reveal His Son in me, that I might preach Him among the Gentiles." Galatians 1:15-16. What a transformation having a Vision makes! Paul would not be detracted from his Vision: "I have run the race set before me." Paul had a goal/Vision set before him. Can you say you are running your race? Are you about your Father's business, doing the Vision He asked you to do?

And again, there was Nehemiah who felt an immense burden when he discovered that the wall of Jerusalem was falling down and its gates had been set on fire. We read that he sat down and wept. He mourned and fasted for days (Nehemiah 1:4). I believe the rebuilding of the wall was a Vision being birthed in Nehemiah. As a cupbearer to King Artaxerxes, being of a sad disposition was not a good look – it could result in your death after all, you were in the presence of the King and all your worries should disappear. However, Nehemiah found favour and not only was he allowed to go to Jerusalem he was able to ask for the resources that he would need to rebuild the wall. When Nehemiah was about His Father's business he would not allow anyone to stop him from doing what he was asked to do by God. So when Sanballat the Horonite, Tobiah the Ammonite and Geshem the Arab heard that the wall was finished they sent word that they wanted to 'chat' (Nehemiah 6:1-17). But Nehemiah knew this was a trick and said no. He knew they wanted to do him harm, so he told them plainly that he was doing a great work. He was totally focused on what he believed God had called him to do.

You may not have heard of Jehoshabeath but you can read about her in 2 Chronicles 22:11. "But Jehoshabeath, the daughter of the king, took Joash the son of Ahaziah, and stole him away from among the king's sons who were being murdered, and put him and his nurse in a bedroom." With no thought for her safety or welfare, because she would have surely been put to death if she was discovered, Jehoshabeath bravely hid him in the bedchamber from Athaliah, so that he was not slain. Now why did she do this? This little-known woman (called Jehosheba in 2 Kings 11:2) had an important place in God's plan of the ages. Through her courage and ingenuity, she preserved the royal line of David through which the Messiah would come. Jehosheba was given a Vision from God and she fulfilled it. I also believe she was moved by compassion.

Perhaps you are familiar with Jehoshebeath, but have you heard of Addisyn Lopez? I came across this woman on Facebook. I haven't met her in person yet, but I believe she is a modern day Jehosheba. I have been struck by her love, compassion and pure joy as she undertakes the Vision God has given her.

As a foster carer and adopter my heart was immediately drawn to Addisyn who is a young woman who was led to start an orphanage called 'Into His Arms', a place for kids diagnosed as terminally ill to be loved until the very end. The first time I heard about her was when I read this on Facebook:

"There's a 10-day-old baby girl and she has a disease," I [Addisyn] was told. "I'll take her," I said without hesitation. Just hours later, the social worker was at our door in Guatemala holding a bundle wrapped in a blanket. She explained the baby was abandoned due to her diagnosis. She was left with nothing, not even a name. And this baby girl wasn't expected to live very long because she had hydranencephaly. She only had about 3% of her brain and an enlarged head due to an abnormal accumulation of fluid in her cranial cavity. The days that followed were filled with MRIs and hospital visits. Then, aged 19-years-old I stood before the judge asking if I could adopt her and give her a name. "Her own family didn't even want her," the judge told me solemnly, "She's probably not going to live, and if she does, she won't have a normal life. Why would you even bother?" I told her I cared because her life matters, and the value of our life isn't decided by the number of our days. I named her Emma Leigh – Emma means 'whole and complete' and Leigh (a middle name I share with my mom) means 'healer.' There were surgeries, court hearings, lost paperwork, and so many medical appointments, but these were never a burden. I just wanted her to be loved here on Earth. Just 31-days-old, Emma Leigh passed from my arms into the arms of Jesus. She was born into a completely hopeless situation but she died being loved. Most children in Guatemala like Emma Leigh are left to die alone. I wasn't okay with that, and could no longer pretend that these kids didn't exist. And so, Into His Arms was born, a place for kids diagnosed as terminally ill to be loved until the very end. Since then, we've cared for and loved many children who had difficult health issues."

As a foster carer of 17 years and counting, I know what it is like to have babies come into my home and heart. Sometimes people would unthinkingly say, "I don't know how you do it, I couldn't. I would be sad to let them go." I never responded – after all, did they think I had no heart? It was indeed sometimes so hard to let them go. Sometimes I felt as

f my heart had been broken and broken again. But the babies that came
nto my care needed to be loved for that time, however long or short.
Whether it was for a week or in some cases years, they needed 100% love
and commitment.

But Addisyn does something I felt I could never do. She took on
children knowing that some of them would not be in this world for long.
I asked God why, and He said that it was because she had a clear Vision
from Him, which she accepted, and if I tried to be someone else it would
totally destroy me. And for those people who feel they can't be a foster carer
or adopter, don't worry – He didn't ask you. But if He did, He would equip
you. You need to know that what you are doing is what God wants you to
do, and not what you believe others want you to do. He will give you the
strength to do His work.

I have had the privilege of meeting many mighty men and women of
God, but none come more to mind that James and Ruth Poach, Pastors
of Regeneration Church in Romford. My daughter had started sailing on
a Sunday (I know some will find that difficult to understand but
perhaps we can talk about that at a later stage!). Anyway, as a family
we wanted to be able to meet together. My eldest daughter, then 15,
wasn't going to church. She had been badly hurt both physically and
emotionally while attending a Christian school, and the idea of church
was not appealing.

One day when walking through my local shopping centre I saw a
group of people singing. My youngest daughter wanted to stop and
listen so we did. When I saw the name I remembered that this was the
church that my son had found accepted him as he was. So we decided to
give it a go. As a family we felt very much at home in the church and
quickly noticed that week after week people spoke to us and welcomed
us. It wasn't a matter of people speaking to us because they were on the
welcome team and after a

few weeks they had 'done their jobs.' No – people here genuinely wanted to get to know us and that was really refreshing.

A facet of Ruth and James' Vision is (in a nutshell) to 'make disciples' who will in turn 'go into the world' and make more disciples. In the time I have known them this is what they have been doing. They have been following the lead of the Holy Spirit very closely. There have been many occasions when James has said, "we are leaning heavily on the Holy Spirit and we are only doing what we believe He wants us to do."

In 2016 there was a prophecy that they would be meeting in a tent! They didn't just discount it but they kept it close to their hearts and who would have known that in 2020 we would have had the coronavirus pandemic and the building that we were meeting in would be unusable and the church would be unable to rent the space. As a result we are meeting in… yes, you guessed it: a marquee. The surroundings are absolutely beautiful and here we will remain until March 2021. Then we will wait until the Holy Spirit tells us where to go next.

Now you may have heard of Dr Thomas John Barnardo. Walking through the streets of Victorian London he was shocked by the appalling conditions the homeless children found themselves in. He wanted to make a difference, and this is what he did. A facet of his Vision was to help the destitute homeless children through education. Dr Barnardo opened his first school in 1867 and the first Boys' Home in 1870. Dr Barnardo opened many homes during his lifetime, and by the time he died in 1905 the charity had opened 96 of them caring for more than 8500 children. This facet lives on, with the Barnardo's Charity continuing to realise his dream of a world where no child is turned away from the help they need.

Dr Barnardo you might have heard of but unless you are a family member or friend or attend my local church, you may never have heard of Dan and Cassie Wicks just two 'ordinary people'. I met them over two years ago when Cassie had just given birth to their daughter, Willow. I remember very clearly them getting up on the stage at church and telling the congregation that they believed God had asked them to go to a Christian village located just outside of Durban, South Africa. They heard and obeyed. They sold everything they had and relocated. Dan and Cassie knew that God would provide for their every need. They got involved with Lungisisa Indlela Village (LIV) in the coastal town of Umhlanga, a residential settlement for vulnerable, parentless children. It has a mission to rescue, raise and educate orphaned children in South Africa. Cassie said she first had a desire to go ever since she did a tour when she was 19. And a few years later she volunteered at an orphanage for rehabilitating glue sniffing children in Kenya. It wasn't until 2017 that she was able to visit the LIV village, at that time she was dating her husband Dan. For years they kept in touch with the village leadership and finally, in December 2020, as a married couple and with a new five month old baby, they moved to South Africa. There are so many people doing what God has asked them to do, and it seems to set them apart. And I am sure you can think of others.

It's as though the Wicks were uniquely created for fulfilling this Vision, and I believe we are all created for a unique purpose. And when you acknowledge that you have been born for a purpose, you are able to focus on what you should be doing: not on what others are doing around you.

CHAPTER 3

Why Do We Need a Vision?

I magine you have been given a gift but for whatever reason you decide not to open it. For many years you keep it and then one day something prompts you to open it. The wrapping has faded and the bow doesn't glisten as much as it did, but nevertheless curiosity has finally got the better of you and you open the gift.

How would you feel if you realised that it would have not only totally changed your life, but also the lives of others? Would you feel hurt or angry or disappointed? To be honest, how you are feeling doesn't really matter. You see, God has already given you a special unique gift. His gift to you is the Vision that He implanted in you, and it doesn't really matter whether you have just discovered it or knew about it years ago, because – starting from now – I believe that with God's help you can be the person He created you to be. But if we do not fulfil the Vision God has called us to be, we perish inwardly and our lives remain unfulfilled, because, "Where there is no revelation, the people cast off restraint; But happy is he who keeps the law. (Proverbs 29:18).

To have a Vision is not enough; in Habakkuk 2:2a it says, "Then the Lord answered me and said: 'Write the vision and make it plain on tablets, that he may run who reads it.'" So you need to write down the Vision, otherwise it will just remain a dream. Having written it down you can then decide the steps that will have to be taken to make it a reality. We don't want to look back in regret, wishing we'd accomplished our Vision. That's not something any of us should have to face.

But what stops us from putting the facets of our Vision down on paper? After all, it's ours: no-one else's. Is it because we are fearful of what others might think? Or are we afraid of failing? Maybe even of achieving it! Now some might say, 'Feel the fear, but do it anyway.' However, God has not given us a spirit of fear, but a spirit of love. So say *no* to fear and "Write the vision and make it plain..." (Habakkuk 2:2).

There should be steps for each facet of your Vision. So being a writer may mean taking a course on creative writing, learning about self-publishing or effective marketing, and so on. To succeed as a friend, it may mean setting aside a certain amount of time each week to visit or call someone, or thinking of ways that might help them, etc. You may want to be a better steward of money. Whatever facets you have, with God's help you can do it.

So straight away you can see the need to manage your time more effectively. Therefore a step would be to plan your week, making sure that you allocate time for those activities that are important. This will force you to prioritise: Jesus was very clear about what He needed to do. He knew that He had been anointed to proclaim The Good News of Salvation. He also knew that He would have to train those who would continue The Way: "And when it was day, He called His disciples to Himself; and from them He chose twelve whom He also named apostles" (Luke 6:13).

In three and a half years Jesus built a ministry that is still growing more than two millennia later. That's being focused! But just how can you be fashioned to focus light that shows your brilliance? The answer is by allowing yourself to be that unique person God created you to be. Then you can finally appreciate just what a miraculous gift you are. And then it really it doesn't matter whether you have kept the gift tucked away for five or even 25 years – starting from now you can be the real You!

Writing down the facets of your Vision will not only give you clarity it also provides you with a goal: something to be achieved and steps to be accomplished. Just like training for a race. You'll find yourself looking forward to it and getting excited rather than worrying about staying the course.

You remember Addisyn Lopez? This is how Jesus called her.

"Do not be afraid to be different from other people. The path I have called you to travel is exquisitely right for you. The more closely you follow My leading, the more fully I can develop your gifts. To follow Me wholeheartedly you must relinquish you desire to please other people. However, your closeness to Me will bless others by enabling you to shine brightly in this dark world."

Listen, a Vision *will* put you in the future and when you live in this truth it will have you shouting from the rooftops!

CHAPTER 4

Fulfilling Your Vision

Do you remember when I said that God rejoices over you? I said it because He can see the end of our lives and He knows what you are! He is faithful and committed to complete the good work that He has started. He knows what He has said to you, and that if He has said it then it will surely come to pass! Now, if God can rejoice over you surely you can as well. If you can't get excited about what God has called you to be, how will others?

And how can I be sure that God knows the person that I really am? Well, I know from Psalm 139:15-16 that says, "My frame was not hidden from You, when I was made in secret, and skilfully wrought in the lowest parts of the earth. Your eyes saw my substance, being yet unformed. And in Your book they all were written, the days fashioned for me, when as yet there were none of them."

The more steps you take towards the realisation of your Vision, the more polished are the facets cut into your character. Then, when you are set in God's purposes the different facets of your character will shine as

God moves in your life. For, "The lamp of the body is the eye. Therefore when your eye is good, your whole body also is full of light" (Luke 11:34a). Therefore the light within you will sparkle more and more as each facet of your life is polished in the quest to realize your Vision.

CHAPTER 5

Staying Close to God

G od uses His words contained in the Bible to impart His wisdom and to give us instructions. If we are to fulfil our purpose, we need to see the end like He does. We need to stay close to God. As He says in His words, we need to abide in Him so He can abide in us. Can fruit flourish and grow on its own? No, it needs the branch. Like the fruit we need Him to flourish and grow, and as you learn to trust God He will help you in the steps you take towards making your Vision a reality. For it is written, "Trust in the Lord with all your heart, and lean not on your own understanding, in all your ways acknowledge Him, and He shall direct your paths" (Proverbs 3:5-6).

Through His Spirit He will reveal
your Vision to you.

When you believe God has revealed to you who He created you to be, lay your Vision and your plans before Him and allow Him to direct your path. As He says in Proverbs 16:9, "A man's heart plans his way, but the Lord directs his steps."

I love Psalm 139. God has fashioned our days for us! He fashioned them when as yet there were none. Hallelujah! To know that God fashioned our days and spoke into our lives, even before we were formed, should be enough for any born-again believer to know that His plans and purpose for our lives are settled in heaven. Now, because He spoke into our lives we can be certain that it will come to pass because, as it says in Isaiah 55 10-11, "So shall My word be that goes forth from My mouth; it shall not return to Me void, but it shall accomplish what I please, and it shall prosper in the thing for which I sent it." So it will accomplish what He pleases, be sure of that.

And we can hold on to this fact.
Glory to God!

Think about it! God the Almighty, the El Shaddai, the All-sufficient One who created Heaven and Earth; who put the stars and the Moon in the sky, who created you and me from dust and spoke into your future. Can there be any doubt that He will make sure you have everything you need? It's true! We do not need to worry, instead we need to first seek the Kingdom of God and as He says all these things shall be added.

So back to where we started – stay close to God! You will become the person He created you to be as you seek the Kingdom of God. Focus on Him and the facets of that Vision will become a reality. When you spend time with Him, reading His word and allowing Him to speak into your very being, He will reveal His word to you. Then, when the storms come, you will not be shaken, because your faith will be built on a solid foundation, just like the wise man in Matthew 7:24-25.

Remember also Philippians 4:6-7, "Be anxious for nothing, but in everything, by prayer and supplication, with thanksgiving, let your requests be made known to God; and the peace of God, which surpasses all understanding, will guard your hearts and minds through Christ Jesus."

The peace of God will come when you spend time with Him. You will know His will for any situation. When fear tries to stop you from doing something, remember that you were not given a spirit of fear but a spirit of love – and perfect loves drives out all fear (2 Timothy 1:7).

Fear can cripple you – it can stop you in your tracks. It can stop you going forward. So, ask God to help you overcome any fear you might experience, such as fear of what people might say, fear of your family, fear of failing or even fear of succeeding. Most of the time we worry needlessly over fears that exist only in our imagination.

> Don't allow fear to stop you being the person
> He created you to be.

Get a notebook, or use my Being Me Journal, available on Amazon, so that each day you can write down how God has blessed you. Also the Being Me Journal will help you with your Vision. This will encourage you when you are going through life's storms. Record the promises that God has made to you so that you can stand on them. As you begin to cherish fulfilled promises your faith cannot but be strengthened. After all, He did it then and He can do it now because He does not change. He cannot! But you've got to exercise your own faith muscles! There's no way you can rely on my faith or the faith of another – it's got to be yours.

CHAPTER 6

Royal Magnificence

We are "…a chosen generation, a royal priesthood, a holy nation, His own special people, that [we] may proclaim the praises of Him who called [us] out of darkness into His marvellous light" (1 Peter 2:9).

It is God's marvellous light that shines upon us and which allows us to shine with such brilliance as His light moves across each facet of our lives. But we must remember that once we, "…who once were not a people but are now the people of God, who had not obtained mercy but now have obtained mercy" (1 Peter 2:10).

In the world, people look upon diamonds as status symbols – objects to be proud of. These people often refer to diamonds as 'rocks.' We must be careful that having been picked out as a gem stone we do not become, "And a stone of stumbling, and a rock of offense" (1 Peter 2:8). However, as long as we believe in the Father and are obedient to The Word, then we can take hold of the promise of Jesus that, "…he who believes in Me, the works that I do he will do also; and greater works than these he will do, because go to My Father. And whatever you ask in My name, that I will do, that the Father may be glorified in the Son" (John 14:12-13).

Yet such magnificence can only be obtained by setting your life in the correct proportions to your natural qualities. This requires the sacrifice of those parts of your life that hinder the beauty within. In this way you are transformed from a rough diamond into one of royal magnificence. In other words, "...do not be conformed to this world, but be transformed by the renewing of your mind, that you may prove what is that good and acceptable and perfect will of God." And by demolishing arguments and, "...casting down arguments and every high thing that exalts itself against the knowledge of God, bringing every thought into captivity to the obedience of Christ" (2 Corinthians 10:5).

But you need to – you've got it – spend time with Him and meditate upon His words so you don't look at what you see in the natural, but what He has to say. In the middle of the coronavirus pandemic in July 2020 I was told that I had cancer and I found that for me meditating on the Bible and spending more time with God really helped and increased my faith. In the natural world I knew I had a diagnosis of cancer but was looking beyond that. Research has shown that when a person looks beyond their diagnosis, they are more likely to get better than when dwelling on their sickness.

Let His word be your final authority.

Then, in the right setting you will be displayed to the best advantage because this will allow God's light to shine through your life.

We need to take a step of faith. *Knowing* what God has called you to be and *being* it is not always easy. Sometimes we want to stay in our present circumstances (going round and round in circles). Why? Because it's comfortable and there is a sense of security in doing what is familiar. When Jesus was walking on the water, just about to pass by the disciples in their storm-tossed boat, Peter cried out to Him, "Lord, if it is you, command me to come to You on the water" (Matthew 14:28). If Jesus commands you, then you need to have the faith to believe that what He has commanded, you can do.

You will only be what you believe you are.

Get out of the boat! As you take the first step of faith your feet will have a solid support in Jesus. You will not sink. Even if you fail Jesus will lift you up, it will be a feat – not a defeat! God says in Jeremiah 33:3, "Call to Me and I will answer you, and show you great and mighty things, which you do not know."

You need to spend time with God discovering the facets that go to make you the person He created you to be. God may have called you to finance different programmes in your community or the world, be a business person, a writer, a homemaker, an usher in your church, a motivational speaker, a gym coach or a friend to lonely people. There is nothing you can't do with God! Put no limit on God's Vision for you.

God knew when He has finished a facet of His Vision. In Genesis 1:31– Genesis 2:1 it says: "Then God saw everything that He had made, and indeed it was very good. So the evening and the morning were the sixth day. Thus the heavens and the earth, and all the host of them, were finished."

With Nehemiah and the task he had of rebuilding the walls surrounding Jerusalem, there was a timescale. As we read in Nehemiah 2:6, Nehemiah gave himself a deadline to complete the task: "Then the king said to me (the queen also sitting beside him), 'How long will your journey be? And when will you return?' So it pleased the king to send me; and I set him a ime." Now had God told Nehemiah how long his task was going to take? There's nothing in the scriptures to suggest this. I believe Nehemiah set . time to force himself to get on with the work that was needed. If we don't set a time, we often let ourselves be distracted because we have no ense of urgency – but Nehemiah was focused, as it is written, "Now it happened when Sanballat, Tobiah, Geshem the Arab, and the rest of our enemies heard that I had rebuilt the wall and that there were no breaks eft in (though at that time I had not hung the doors in the gates), that Sanballat and Geshem sent to me, saying, 'Come, let us meet together among the villages in the plain of Ono.' But they thought to do me harm. So I sent messengers to them, saying, 'I am doing a great work, so that I cannot come down. Why should the work cease while I leave it and go down to you?' But they sent me this message four times, and I answered them in the same manner" (Nehemiah 6:1-3). But again in the same way that facets can be added to our lives, not all facets have deadlines.

Jesus knew when he had finished a facet of His Vision, for in John 19:30 it says, "So when Jesus had received the sour wine, He said 'It is finished!' And bowing His head, He gave up His spirit."

Paul also knew when he said, "I have fought the good faith, I have finished the race, I have kept the faith" (2 Timothy 4:7-8). It is the same with your Vision; you need to know the different facets of your Vision and their deadlines. However, we still need to break them down further to make each one more manageable.

Now, we've already discussed God's timescale for realising His Vision for creation. He set Himself six days, with each day having a goal to be accomplished. So we too should give ourselves realistic timescales with manageable goals. Once you've written down your goals break them down into steps that need to be done to accomplish each particular goal.

> Remember, to climb the stairs all it takes
> is one step at a time.

Write down as many steps that you feel you need to take. You migh
wonder why I keep asking you to write things down. It's because if yo
don't you will forget! Remember, it is your Vision and it's important to fin
the way for recording your Vision that will enable you to complete the tas
set before you.

Pray with your understanding and pray in your heavenly language
Remember the passage quoted earlier, "Eye has not seen, nor ear heard, no
have entered into the heart of man, the things which God has prepared fo
those who love Him" (1 Corinthians 2:10). God has promised to establish
your works and through His Spirit He will reveal to you the steps needec
to carry out the task that will accomplish your goals and ultimately you
Vision. Sometimes all we will get from God is the next step – take it in
faith! That's all we need!

CHAPTER 7

The Beginning - Omega

This is the beginning and what you do now is up to you. You have your Vision before you and have sought the Lord. Do not put this gift away again, use it and live life the way God intended. In abundance, for He says, "I have come that they might have life and that they might have it more abundantly" (John 10:10b).

Don't let go of this Vision that God has put inside you. Put the facets and steps of your Vision in a place where you can reach them easily and refer to them as often as you need to.

Every new day that you wake up to should be an exciting one, because each day with God is taking you a step towards being the person He created you to be. We are going from one degree of glory to another. How do I know that? Because He says so in His word.

My prayer for you is that you become the person that God created you to be.

What would you do if you knew you couldn't fail?

Wow, that's amazing!

Now go do it.

You can only become what you already are.

And Now
The Final Word.....

I was talking to a friend of mine and she said, 'I don't believe I have a purpose.' And I asked her what she did at the moment and she said she was a school teacher, a mother, a wife, friend and neighbour. So, I said I believe that God wants you to start where you're at. Think, how do you become a better schoolteacher (allow God to polish that facet), how do you become a better mother, (allow God to polish that facet), how do you become a better friend? You've got it – allow God to polish that facet. And I know as you do the things that God has already asked you to do He will ask you to do more things. A better neighbour? God will give you ways to become better. One friend told me that before lockdown she and her husband had a 'tea party' for their neighbours. And she can't wait to have more. As it says in Luke 16:10, "He who is faithful in what is least is faithful also in much; and he who is unjust in what is least is unjust also in much."

I have known Helen Yousaf for over 28 years now, and as well as being a very talented musician she also has an amazing artistic talent. I remember when I first met her there were times when she would be painting the

scenes for a play that the church was performing. Now her paintings ar
absolutely breath-taking and during the pandemic there were displayed i
hospitals all over the UK, and I know it gave people hope.

So, start where you are at.

Sample Facets
of My Vision

These are two of my facets that I am working on – yours will be different

Facet – To develop a closer relationship with God
- Step 1 – Read the Bible daily, spending time to meditate on the word
- Step 2 – Find a local church
- Step 3 – Listen to podcasts
- Step 4 – Watch YouTube videos

These are only a few of the steps there are other steps, but if this is what you want, make it personal to you.

Facet – To become a proficient investor
- Step 1 – Shares, Forex, options, futures? Which asset?
- Step 2 – Find training courses relevant to my chosen asset
- Step 3 – Enrol on training course
- Step 4 – Practice and practice, then practice some more until I am confident to place trades

Again, there are other steps, but if this is what you want to do you need to decide your own steps that suit you best.

Remember our life with God is a like a journey, so keep a journal or use the 'Being Me Journal' which is available on amazon.

It will help your faith as you look back and see answers to prayers.

For more information on Addisyn Lopez visit
https://villageofhopeguatemala.com/about/lopez-family/ or find her on
Facebook https://www.facebook.com/addisyn.block

For more information on LIV Village where Dan and Cassie Wicks are
volunteers work visit https://www.liv-village.com/

For Helen Yousaf's shop visit
www.helen-yousaf-art.com

The Joy of Being Me Journal is available on amazon

Printed in Great Britain
by Amazon